THE WORLD HERITAGE

THE CHINESE EMPIRE

UNESCO

CHILDRENS PRESS ®

CHICAGO

Table of Contents

Library of Congress Cataloging-in-Publication Data
Terzi, Marinella.
    [Imperio Chino. English]
    The Chinese Empire / by Marinella Terzi.
        p.   cm. — (The World heritage)
    Translation of: El Imperio Chino.
    Includes index.
    Discusses the culture of China over a period of four thousand years and examines
some of the structures and artwork that remain from that civilization.
    ISBN 0-516-08377-5
    1. China — History — Juvenile literature. [1. China — Civilization. 2. China —
Antiquities.] I. Title. II. Series.
DS736.T45 1992
951 — dc20
                                                                                92-7509
                                                                                CIP
                                                                                AC

El Imperio Chino: © INCAFO S.A./Ediciones S.M./UNESCO 1990
The Chinese Empire: © Childrens Press, Inc./UNESCO 1992

ISBN (UNESCO) 92-3-102594-5
ISBN (Childrens Press) 0-516-08377-5

The Chinese Empire

The People's Republic of China is one of the largest nations in the world. It covers an area of 3,691,500 square miles (9,561,000 square kilometers). Over one billion people live within its borders, more than in any other country. This is about one out of every five people in the world.

Because its land is so vast, China has not become too crowded. But it has had to adopt a distinctive way of life. The Chinese economy depends a great deal on agriculture. Rice, wheat, and cotton are the main crops. About four-fifths of the people live in rural areas.

Chinese history reaches back more than four thousand years. For most of that time, the country has stood apart from the rest of the world. This isolation is largely due to China's natural boundaries. To the north are the Mongolian steppes and the Gobi Desert. The Tibetan plateaus and the mountain ranges of Yunnan and Sichuan provinces lie to the west and south. On the south and east is the Pacific Ocean.

But China was never too concerned about being isolated. In fact, it was partly a matter of choice. For centuries, China considered itself the center of the universe and provided for all its own needs. Because it stood alone, China developed a unique culture—one very different from its neighbors.

Isolated from the World

China remained out of touch with the rest of the world during most of its four-thousand-year history. Its boundaries were natural barriers. But this was not a problem; China was well able to take care of itself. In its own eyes, China was the center of the universe. It was indeed a fortress, becoming even stronger after the Great Wall was built. The top photo shows the Great Wall's eastern end, known as Laolongtou, or Old Dragon Head, at Shanhaiguan. The photo below shows part of the Forbidden City in Beijing.

4

Dynasty after Dynasty

Chinese society was a society of classes from earliest times. The common people were mostly poor farmers. For thousands of years they were oppressed by the powerful: by governments, landlords, bandits, and money lenders.

At times during China's history, some of the peasants were tenant farmers. Tenants had to give a large portion of their harvests to the landlord, who also charged them high rents. For everyone, tenants and landowners alike, taxes were high. Farms were small, and food could be very scarce. Many peasants barely had enough to eat. Thus, when they were not tending their fields, they often looked for other work.

End of a Legend

One day in 1974, three farmers were digging a well in the ground near Mount Lishan. Suddenly the earth cracked open and an army of terra cotta soldiers appeared beneath them. What had been a legend — the Mausoleum of Shi Huangdi — was now reality. The soldier at the right is one of the many figures found, each one with a different face. His clothes reveal the military style of his time. At the left is the fortress known as The Gateway, which lies north of the Great Wall. Restoration of it began in 1949.

The Forbidden City

The Imperial Palace at Beijing was called the Forbidden City because ordinary citizens were not allowed to enter it. The most terrible curse befell any commoner who dared to cross its boundaries. After the last emperor, Pu Yi, was forced to give up his throne, the palace lost its aura of mystery. Eventually it was opened to the public. Every emperor of the Qing Dynasty and a great many emperors of the Ming Dynasty lived there. The Forbidden City is a complex of many buildings, with a total of more than nine thousand rooms. This photo shows the Hall of Supreme Harmony, or Taihe.

Hunting, fishing, and working as craftsmen or servants added to their income. Even today, many Chinese peasants still do these things.

With little food and many mouths to feed, some families were forced to sell their children. Boys were sent to become novices in monasteries or servants at court or in private homes. Girls were sold as servants or entertainers.

The country's climate and intricate, mountainous terrain added more hardships. Throughout their history, the Chinese had to deal with floods, droughts, and wars.

A feudal system was created during the Zhou Dynasty (1122 B.C. to 221 B.C.). Under feudalism, political authority was spread out among many feudal lords. Little by little, this system was replaced by a central government, and the idea of a single emperor took root.

The first emperor was Shi Huangdi. He built a mausoleum that for many centuries was thought to be just a legend. Shi Huangdi founded the Qin Dynasty (221 B.C. to 206 B.C.), put an end to feudalism, and unified China.

Under the Han Dynasty (202 B.C. to A.D. 220), China still held together as a unified state. Through good economic policies, the empire prospered.

One of the most brilliant periods in the nation's history began under the Tang Dynasty, lasting from A.D. 618 to 907. China then rose to become the political, economic, and cultural center of all Asia.

Total anarchy swept China during the period of the Five Dynasties (907 to 960). Then the Song Dynasty (960 to 1279) unified the country once again.

People's Republic of China

The People's Republic of China is 3,691,500 square miles (9,561,000 square kilometers) in area, making it one of the world's largest nations. It has the greatest population of any country—more than one billion people, or one out of every five people in the world. On this map can be found three of the sites that UNESCO has chosen as part of the World Heritage: the Great Wall, the Mausoleum of Shi Huangdi, and the Imperial Palace in Beijing.

Protection from Barbarians

The Great Wall was built to defend China against invaders from the north, whom the Chinese called barbarians. The wall today is more than 4,000 miles (6,400 kilometers) long, from the Gulf of Bohai in the east to Gansu province in north-central China. This photo shows a restored portion in the area of Shanhaiguan. At the left is a decorative wooden detail, painted in many colors, over one of the doorways at the Imperial Palace, Beijing.

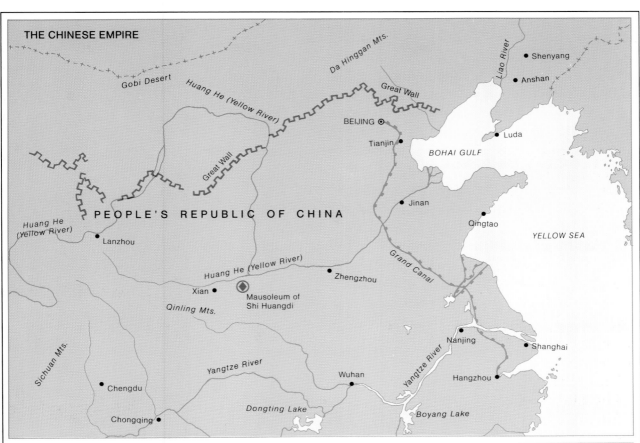

THE CHINESE EMPIRE

Gobi Desert
Huang He (Yellow River)
Da Hinggan Mts.
Great Wall
Liao River
Shenyang
Anshan
Great Wall
BEIJING ⊙
Tianjin
Luda
BOHAI GULF
Huang He (Yellow River)
Great Wall
PEOPLE'S REPUBLIC OF CHINA
Jinan
Huang He (Yellow River)
Lanzhou
Qingtao
YELLOW SEA
Huang He (Yellow River)
Zhengzhou
Xian
Mausoleum of Shi Huangdi
Grand Canal
Qinling Mts.
Nanjing
Shanghai
Sichuan Mts.
Yangtze River
Wuhan
Yangtze River
Hangzhou
Chengdu
Dongting Lake
Boyang Lake
Chongqing

The Mongols invaded China in the thirteenth century, taking over the city that is now Beijing. Kublai Khan (1215–1295), grandson of the great conqueror Genghis Khan, founded the capital of the Mongol Empire there. Marco Polo, a traveler from Venice, became a personal friend of the Great Khan. Acting as Kublai's ambassador, he visited far corners of the Mongol Empire. This was the first time that many Chinese people, isolated for so long, looked upon the facial features of someone from the West.

In 1352 a Buddhist monk led an uprising against the Mongols. This monk was Hongwu, first emperor of the Ming Dynasty (1368 to 1644). The Imperial Palace was built during the Ming Dynasty. So was most of the Great Wall.

China at last opened its doors to the West during the Ming period. The first Portuguese ship arrived in 1514. In 1557, the Portuguese founded the colony of Macao on the Chinese mainland. Dutch, English, and Spanish ships followed.

How Do the Chinese Write?

The Chinese language is monosyllabic—that is, made up of single syllables. Mandarin Chinese, the dialect spoken in Beijing, is composed of 62 monosyllabic sounds. Most words in spoken Chinese are one-syllable. Many, however, are compounds made by combining two or more monosyllables in various ways.

In Mandarin, each monosyllable can be pronounced in four different tones, or pitches. At each tone level, the word has a different meaning.

Each region of China has its own spoken dialect. While they all use the same words, each region follows different tone patterns. There are hundreds of Chinese dialects, and some use as many as nine tones. Thus, only people from the same region can understand each other.

Now the Chinese government is trying to establish a common language that will be understood by all Chinese people. This language is based on Mandarin Chinese.

While the spoken language differs throughout the country, written Chinese is the same for all. Instead of an alphabet, there are characters. The number of characters in written Chinese is much higher than the number of spoken monosyllables. A large Chinese dictionary may contain 40,000 to 50,000 characters. A person has to know about 5,000 characters to read a Chinese newspaper.

Each Chinese monosyllable is written as a single character. The earliest Chinese writing consisted of pictographs. These were characters that resembled the objects they stood for.

Ideographs and compound ideographs are other types of Chinese characters. These represent concepts, qualities, or combinations of ideas. Some characters are "borrowed" from words having the same sound but different meaning. Still other characters are known as phonetic compounds. These characters include a pronunciation symbol to show which of a word's several meanings is intended.

Calligraphy—elegant, artistic handwriting—was considered a high art during the Chinese Empire. The Six Virtues for noblemen were archery, horsemanship, social and religious rituals, music, mathematics—and calligraphy. Calligraphy is still a respected art in China today. Now, as in the past, calligraphers dedicate long hours to their art, working with a brush and black ink.

When Chinese is written in the Western alphabet, it is said to be "romanized." There are two major styles of romanization, Wade-Giles and pinyin. This is why we see different spellings of the same Chinese word. For instance, "Peking" is the Wade-Giles form of China's capital, and "Beijing" is the pinyin form. In 1978, the Chinese government declared pinyin to be the official romanization for the Chinese language.

Building on a Grand Scale

Architecture in China has always been on the grand scale, reflecting the dimensions of the country itself. *(Top)* One of the courtyards between palace residences inside the Forbidden City. *(Bottom)* Visitors walking along the Great Wall in the area of Badaling.

Jesuit missionaries, who first entered China in the 1500s, became great mediators between the Chinese and westerners. The Jesuits had a strong scholarly background. They were respected in the Chinese court because they were experts in mathematics and in casting almanacs. Granted this respect, they were free to carry out their spiritual missions.

The Qing Dynasty (1644 to 1911) was China's last. Like the period of Mongol rule, the Qing was a regime of outsiders. This time it was the Manchus to the northeast who invaded China. The Qing Dynasty was brought to an end by Sun Yat-sen's revolution of 1911.

Religion and Art

Many religions and philosophies were practiced in traditional China. The most prominent were Confucianism, Daoism (Taoism), and Buddhism. Confucius (551 to 479 B.C.) advocated loyalty, order, and respect. His philosophy was based on the principle of *ren*—compassion and human kindness. Those searching for wisdom must submit their will to the natural order, the way—*dao*—of heaven.

Love for one's ancestors was basic for Confucius. This idea follows the Chinese tradition that associates old age with wisdom. Mao Zedong's revolution of 1949 stamped out the teaching of Confucianism.

Lao Zi (sixth century B.C.) was the founder of Daoism. Its ideas are set forth in the *Dao De Jing (Tao Te Ching)*. According to Lao Zi, a person is only a part of nature and must blend with it completely. The universe follows the principles of *yin* and *yang*. *Yin* is the feminine force, and *yang* is the masculine.

The Ideal of Chinese Art

The exquisite art of China remained unknown in the West until Europeans began traveling to China. By the 1700s, traffic was flowing freely between East and West. The decorative style of Eastern lands became the height of European fashion. No European palace of that period was considered fashionable unless it included at least one Chinese room. But the only true Chinese art is that of China itself. In the top photo is a turtle outside the Hall of Supreme Harmony. Below it is the interior of the Union Hall or Jiaotai, where empresses were crowned and their birthdays celebrated.

Soldiers Marching Out of the Ground

Since the Mausoleum of Shi Huangdi was discovered in 1974, archaeologists have continued to excavate. More than seven thousand soldiers have already been unearthed. Though little of the paint remains on the statues, we know that their uniforms were originally multi-colored.

The symbol for Daoism represents the union of the two principles. It is a circle divided into two sections, a dark part *(yin)* and a light part *(yang)*. Each part contains a dot of its opposite. Surrounding the circle are the eight elements: sky, earth, thunder, air, water, fire, mountain, and lake.

Buddhism was borrowed from India, where it was born. It came to China via the Silk Road—a traders' route—around the second century A.D.

The Chinese excelled in the "arts of the brush"—calligraphy, poetry, and painting. Each brushstroke reveals the refined nature of the Chinese soul. The Chinese also created works in silk, porcelain, lacquer, and jade. They used these decorative materials to beautify their clothing and their homes.

Many Chinese temples, monasteries, and shrines of brick, stone, and wood are still standing. Some were built by emperors; others, by private citizens. Some still attract devout Buddhists, Daoists, or Confucianists, who come to meditate or pray as they have for centuries. The earliest surviving temples date from the eighth to ninth centuries A.D. Numerous temples remain from the Song, Yuan, and Ming periods.

Drama reached a high point in Imperial China. Music served as a background for stage shows, and female roles were played by men.

Roots of Chinese Wisdom

Buddhism: a philosophy begun in India by Siddhartha Gautama in the sixth century B.C. It teaches freedom from life's misery through purity of mind and soul.

Confucianism: a moral and political doctrine founded by Confucius in the sixth century B.C. and practiced by Chinese, Japanese, and Koreans

Dao (or Tao): the way of heaven

Daoism (or Taoism): a philosophy and religion believed to have originated with Lao Zi. Its symbol is the union of yin and yang.

Ren: in Confucianism, the principle of compassion and human kindness

Yang: the masculine, active principle in Daoism

Yin: the feminine, passive principle in Daoism

The Guardian Lion

A unique feature of Chinese sculpture is its treatment of animals. The figure in this photo is part dog, part lion. The English term for this kind of guardian animal is "Fu-dog." The Chinese call them lions. This sculpture stands among the palaces on the west side of the Forbidden City. Made of bronze, it is one of 12,000 different sculptures, all of them restored, found at the Imperial Palace. Notice how perfectly the animal's muscles are formed and how fierce its face looks—truly a guardian lion.

The Chinese were great inventors. The West imported paper, gunpowder, and printed pictures from the Chinese, as well as tea, oranges, and some garden flowers. Even something as Italian as pasta is said to have been introduced to Italy by Marco Polo, who learned about it in China.

The Chinese were also master cartographers, or mapmakers. Until well into the seventeenth century, their maps were much more accurate than those produced in the West. During the Qing Dynasty the Chinese, learning from the Jesuits, began to apply European techniques to map drawing.

China's exquisite art remained unknown in the West until Europeans began traveling to China. Then it flowed to the West, where Eastern art became the height of fashion in the 1700s. No palace of that period was considered complete unless it had at least one Chinese room.

The Great Wall

How could the Chinese tackle a building project as tremendous as the Great Wall? The answer lies in the nature and attitudes of the Chinese people. They were confident of their power, and they were aware of the vastness of their land. They had to protect themselves in any way they could against invasions by people from the north. So they were determined to build a wall, even though it would have to extend more than 4,000 miles (6,400 kilometers).

The Great Wall, as it stands now, was preceded by structures built even before the third century B.C. Under orders of the first emperor, Shi Huangdi, laborers linked the remains of old fortresses. These had been built in the northern states for defense against the Xiongnu. Thus the first wall appeared, longer than the wall we see today.

Emperor Shi Huangdi abolished feudalism and established the first Chinese empire. But his reign was tyrannical. He did not hesitate to order a murder if he thought someone stood in the way of his goals. And he readily used prisoners to build his wall—a solid wall that reflected China's idea of itself as the center of the universe. In only nine years, from 215 B.C. to 206 B.C., 1,550 miles (2,500 kilometers) of the wall were built.

During the next dynasty, the Han (206 B.C. to A.D. 220), more building was done. Lookout towers were added to the wall every 1.5 miles (2.5 kilometers), guard posts every 3 miles (5 kilometers), fortresses every 9 miles (15 kilometers), and barracks every 31 miles (50 kilometers).

Symbol of Daoism

Daoist Symbols

The drawing above shows the symbol for Daoism, a union of the *yin*, or feminine principle (dark part), and the *yang*, or masculine principle (light part). Each part contains a dot of its opposite, since nothing is absolute. The circle is surrounded by the eight elements: sky, earth, thunder, air, water, fire, mountain, and lake. According to Lao Zi, the founder of Daoism, the symbol represents the order of the universe. The top photo on the opposite page is a reconstructed section of the Great Wall in Shanhaiguan. Below, a fortress in the same place.

With the fall of the Han Dynasty, China again fell into confusion and chaos. Internal fighting plagued the country. The wall gradually crumbled. No one took any interest in it until the 1300s, when the Ming emperors reigned.

Once the Mongols were expelled, the Ming emperors began to reconstruct the wall. In effect, they had to build it all over again, since it had practically been destroyed. They erected some 3,500 more miles (5,650 kilometers) of wall, adding 25,000 towers and 15,000 fortresses.

The Great Wall is built of stone, bricks, and pounded earth. It extends from the Gulf of Bohai in the east to Gansu province in north-central China. It actually consists of two parallel walls, some 10 meters (about 33 feet) high, topped by a wide paved road. A huge monument stands at each end of the wall. The one in the east is named "First Pass under Heaven," and the one in the west is "Last Pass under Heaven."

The Great Wall played more than a protective role. It was also a road for rapid communications. Imperial messengers traveled this route in times of peace. It had an important cultural function, too. It marked the boundary between civilized China and the "barbarian" land to the north.

The Great Wall is spectacular to see. It is striking not only for its length, but also for the perfect way it fits into its natural surroundings. It follows the outline of mountains so perfectly that parts of the wall run almost straight up and down.

The Work of Different Dynasties

The Great Wall was preceded by structures dating back before the third century B.C. Forced laborers, under the orders of emperor Shi Huangdi, worked to join up remnants of still earlier fortresses. But it was the Ming Dynasty, in the fourteenth century A.D., that built the present wall. *(Top left)* A section of the wall not yet restored. *(Top right)* A statue at the wall's eastern end. *(Bottom)* A restored part of the Great Wall at Shanhaiguan.

Chinese Characters

The anonymous builders of the Great Wall have earned the respect of all humanity. This respect deepened when astronauts Neil Armstrong and Edwin Aldrin made the first moon landing on July 21, 1969. As they looked back to Earth, they could make out a very fine, winding line in Asia. It was the Great Wall of China, the only work made by human hands that could be identified from the moon.

The Mausoleum of Shi Huangdi

Emperor Shi Huangdi was certainly a unique character. He did unify China, but he also became drunk with power. Once he attained the imperial throne, he became obsessed with immortality. He hoped never to die. Astrologers, magicians, and sorcerers were summoned to his court. Yet all these wise men made no difference. Shi Huangdi died anyway, when he was only fifty years old. But before his death he ordered a fabulous mausoleum to be built.

The historian Sima Qian (145 to 90 B.C.) described the mausoleum in his writings. He reported that 700,000 artisans worked on its interior. Precious metals and jewels adorned the tomb, he wrote, and rivers of mercury flowed through it. Gold and silver birds perched in jade pine trees, and glistening pearls studded the ceiling, tracing the constellations. The Mausoleum of Shi Huangdi became a legend that grew more fantastic as time went by. Stories about the tomb were passed from parent to child, yet no trace of it had ever been found.

Until 1974, that is. That year, three farmers were digging a well in the ground near Mount Lishan. Suddenly the earth cracked open. Under their feet an army of terra cotta figures appeared. The legend of Shi Huangdi's mausoleum was reality once again.

The mausoleum mound — the emperor's burial chamber — is square in plan, rising 250 feet (76 meters) high. It lies within a complex covering almost 22 square miles (56 square kilometers). The mound itself has not been excavated yet, but archaeologists now understand the area around it.

A square wall surrounds the mound, and another wall surrounds that one. In each wall are four entrances facing the four points of the compass. Beyond the outer wall is a chamber of bronze chariots, each drawn by four horses. Another site is a cemetery of the royal stable, where chariots and horses were buried. Nearby are burial sites of sacrificed generals. In yet another pit lie the remains of workers who helped build the mausoleum. All of them were sacrificed.

The First Emperor's Mausoleum

China's first emperor, Shi Huangdi, struggled all his life to achieve immortality. Inevitably, he failed. He died when he was only fifty years old. But he did live to order the building of a magnificent mausoleum. In all, it covers an area of almost 22 square miles (56 square kilometers). Near the burial chamber are two cemeteries. One is for workers who built the mausoleum, and the other is for generals and for chariots and horses of the royal stable. The most famous feature, however, is the army of terra cotta figures, shown in the three photos at the right.

In Harmony with Nature

The Great Wall is an amazing sight. It is remarkable not only for its length, but also for the way it adapts to nature. Where a mountain slope is very steep, so too is the wall. At times, it is almost vertical. The main function of the Great Wall was protection. But it was also a means for moving goods and messages quickly, thanks to the avenue along the top. It was wide enough for typical carts hauling farm products. Imperial messengers traveled this road and, in times of war, troops marched along it. At right is a view of the Great Wall in the mountainous area of Badaling.

But the most striking feature of the mausoleum compound is its army of terra cotta soldiers. In a vast chamber stand the 7,000 warriors in battle formation; almost all were armed with spears, bows, or swords. But most of their weapons were made of wood and have not survived. The same is true of the chariots pulled by the terra cotta horses.

The soldiers were portrayed as a realistic army. By studying them closely, we can learn much about Chinese military practices in Shi Huangdi's time. Remarkably, all the statues have different faces and different heights. Some observers believe they are exact copies of actual soldiers of the time. The soldiers' uniforms were painted, and each battalion had its own color. Only traces of the paint remain today.

It appears that the soldiers nearest to the entrance carried crossbows loaded with real arrows. A clever mechanism would automatically shoot the arrows at any intruder who dared to enter the tomb.

The Mausoleum of Shi Huangdi is the largest underground site preserved in China. In its structure, it resembles the layout of the emperor's capital city.

The Imperial Palace of the Ming and Qing Dynasties

The Imperial Palace complex in Beijing is also known as the Forbidden City. Completed in 1420, it was the home of emperors of the Ming and Qing Dynasties for over 500 years.

The Forbidden City measures about one-half mile by three-quarters of a mile (.8 kilometers by 1.2 kilometers). It is surrounded by a moat 170 feet (52 meters) wide and a wall 35 feet (11 meters) high.

The city where Beijing now stands became China's capital during the time of the Mongol emperor Kublai Khan. The Mongols called the city Dadu, but in the West it was known as Cambaluc, and later as Peking. The city had a perfectly square ground plan. It was divided into two sections: the inner, forbidden city, seat of royalty; and the outer city, where the ordinary people lived.

All that is left of the old Mongol city are a few remnants of its walls. In 1368, the Chinese succeeded in expelling the Mongols, whom they had always considered intruders. The capital was moved to Nanjing. But emperor Yongle — son of the first Ming, Hongwu — moved it back to the site of Beijing. It was under his orders that the Imperial Palace was built.

The Order of Heaven

The Imperial Palace in Beijing was built under the orders of Emperor Yongle. It is laid out in a rectangular plan, like the capital city itself. This design suggested the order of heaven for the Chinese. The palace complex is composed of two sections. The outer part was devoted to public life, and the inner part was reserved for the private quarters of the imperial family. The palace grounds cover an area of 720,000 square meters, or more than a quarter of a square mile. A moat 170 feet (52 meters) wide and a wall 35 feet (11 meters) high surround it. *(Top photo)* A room at the Hall for Mind Cultivation, the emperor's study. *(Below)* The entrance to the Hall of Heavenly Purity, where the emperor lived.

The immense palace complex—there are more than nine thousand rooms altogether—follows a rectangular plan. All the important halls are lined up along a north-south axis. Marble, lacquered wood, and glazed ceramics are the main construction materials.

There are two sections in the Forbidden City—the outer court to the south and the inner court to the north. The southern part was the seat of public life. There the emperor carried out his official and ceremonial duties. In the northern, or inner, court are the royal family's private quarters.

This plan was not chosen in a careless way, but for good reason. To the Chinese, it represented the order of heaven.

Beyond the main courtyard at the entrance of the Forbidden City are the three most important buildings for the emperor's official business. The southernmost one is the Hall of Supreme Harmony, the largest, best-preserved structure of them all. This was the throne room and the site of important imperial events.

Next is the Hall of Perfect Harmony, where the emperor received visitors. The northernmost is the Hall for Preserving Harmony, where official banquets were held.

The most important building of the inner court is the Hall of Heavenly Purity, where the emperor lived. Around it are pavilions for the empress, the concubines, and the emperor's children.

Magnificent Beijing

The beautiful Imperial Palace rose in Beijing, a city once admired for its beauty by Marco Polo. The buildings made liberal use of marble, lacquered wood, and glazed ceramics. This luxurious decoration reached its peak in the rooms of the Imperial Palace. The top photo shows the entryway to one of the many halls. Below is the Gate of Heavenly Peace (Tiananmen), the main entrance to the Imperial City, within which is the Forbidden City.

Timeline of Chinese History

(Some reigns overlap.)

23rd–18th century B.C.	Xia Dynasty
18th–12th century B.C.	Shang Dynasty
1122 B.C.–221 B.C.	Zhou Dynasty
221 B.C.–206 B.C.	Qin Dynasty; construction of the Mausoleum of Shi Huangdi
202 B.C.–A.D. 220	Han Dynasty
220–280	Period of the Three Kingdoms
265–420	Jin Dynasty
301–589	Northern and Southern Dynasties
581–618	Sui Dynasty
618–907	Tang Dynasty
907–960	Period of the Five Dynasties
960–1279	Song Dynasty
1279–1368	Mongolian (Yuan) Dynasty
1368–1644	Ming Dynasty; construction of Great Wall and Imperial Palace
1644–1911	Qing Dynasty
1911	Sun Yat-sen Revolution
1949	Mao Zedong Revolution

The Imperial Palace was the residence of the court for almost five centuries. During all those years, the common people were prohibited from crossing the great moat and wall and entering the Forbidden City. A most dreadful curse would fall on anyone who dared enter.

The last emperor of the Qing Dynasty, Pu Yi, was forced to give up his throne in February 1912. He was nevertheless allowed to stay on at the palace.

Pu Yi, the loneliest of emperors, abandoned his imperial residence in 1924 and went to Manchuria in the northeast. This was the ancestral home of the Manchu invaders who had founded the Qing Dynasty. The Forbidden City soon lost its aura of mystery and was eventually opened to the public.

Landmarks of History

China has produced countless works of art throughout its four-thousand-year history. Six of them have been included so far on UNESCO's World Heritage list. Details on the opposite page: *(Left)* The army in the Mausoleum of Shi Huangdi. *(Top right)* The Forbidden City's Meridian Gate (Wumen). *(Bottom right)* The gate at Shanhaiguan, the east end of the Great Wall, known as Laolongtou or Old Dragon Head. China's other World Heritage sites (not shown) are the Peking Man site at Zhoukouzhen, Mount Taishan, and the Mogao Caves.

The Art of Bronze

Chinese artists were very skillful at molding bronze. Most of the sculptures at the Imperial Palace are made of this metal. The bronze incense burner shown here is located in the Western Quarter of the palace's inner court.

These Sites Are Part of the World Heritage

The Great Wall was built in the fourteenth century under the Ming Dynasty, though its outline dates back to the third century B.C. It extends more than 4,000 miles (6,400 kilometers) from the Gulf of Bohai to Gansu province. The wall was erected as a defense against "barbarian" invaders from the north. It also served as a means of communication, by way of the paved road along the top.

The Mausoleum of Shi Huangdi. The first Chinese emperor, founder of the Qin Dynasty, ordered the construction of his own mausoleum in the third century B.C. Besides the emperor's burial chamber, the complex has at least two cemeteries and a formidable army of 7,000 life-size terra cotta soldiers. Three peasants discovered the mausoleum in 1974.

The Imperial Palace of the Ming and Qing Dynasties in Beijing was completed in 1420. Chinese emperors lived there until 1924, when the last emperor, Pu Yi, abandoned it. It covers an area of .28 square mile (720,000 square meters) and is surrounded by a moat 170 feet (52 meters) wide and a 35-foot (11-meter) wall. The outer section was for the emperor's public life, while the inner section housed the imperial family's private quarters. The palace complex has more than nine thousand rooms.

Glossary

almanac: a calendar giving predictions of the weather and of astronomical conditions for each day of the year

anarchy: disorder due to the absence of a central ruler or government

ancestors: forefathers; people from whom you are descended

anonymous: nameless; unknown by name

archaeologist: a scientist who learns about the past by studying ancient objects, buildings, or monuments

aura: a special feeling surrounding something

calligraphy: the art of beautiful handwriting

ceramics: pottery or decorations made from baked clay

concubines: women kept in a palace to entertain a ruler

constellations: outlines or patterns that stars and planets seem to form in the sky

dynasty: a family of rulers who pass their leadership down to family members

excavate: to dig up out of the ground

exquisite: beautifully crafted, perfect, delicate

feudalism: a system in which nobles own much of a country's land, and commoners swear loyalty to them and pay a fee to live on the land

ideograph: a character or symbol in some written languages that stands for an object or idea, instead of representing the sound of a word

imperial: having to do with emperors or empires

isolated: separated or removed from others

lacquered: coated with a hard, shiny varnish

legend: a fabulous story from the past

mausoleum: a large, often ornate, tomb

mediator: a middleman; someone who makes peace or carries messages between two parties

moat: a wide ditch or river dug around a city or castle to protect it from invaders

monastery: a house for monks or other people who have taken religious vows

novice: someone beginning his or her training in a religious community

pavilion: a tent, canopy, or decorative building used for shelter or entertainment

restoration: the act of returning something to its original condition

terra cotta: a type of baked clay

tyrannical: using one's power in a cruel way

Index

Page numbers in boldface type indicate illustrations.

Titles in the World Heritage Series

The Land of the Pharaohs
The Chinese Empire
Ancient Greece
Prehistoric Rock Art
The Roman Empire
Mayan Civilization
Tropical Rain Forests
Inca Civilization
Prehistoric Stone Monuments
Romanesque Art and Architecture
Great Animal Refuges of the World
Coral Reefs

Photo Credits

Cover: J. de Vergara/Incafo; p. 3: Incafo; pp. 5 and 6: J. de Vergara/Incafo; p. 7: Incafo; pp. 8,9,10,11, and 13: J. de Vergara/Incafo; p. 14: Incafo; p. 15: J. de Vergara/ Incafo, Incafo; pp. 17, 19, and 21: J. de Vergara/Incafo; p. 23: Incafo; pp. 24-25: J. de Vergara/Incafo; p. 27: Incafo, J. de Vergara/Incafo; pp. 29 and 30: J. de Vergara/ Incafo; p. 31: Incafo, J. de Vergara/Incafo; back cover: Incafo, J. de Vergara/Incafo.

Project Editor, Childrens Press: Ann Heinrichs
Original Text: Marinella Terzi
Subject Consultant: Dr. Chuimei Ho
Translator: Angela Ruiz
Design: Alberto Caffaratto
Cartography: Modesto Arregui
Drawings: Federico Delicado
Phototypesetting: Publishers Typesetters, Inc.